MW00343837

The 3-D Library of the Human Body

THE HEAD AND NECK

LEARNING HOW WE USE OUR MUSCLES

Walter Oleksy

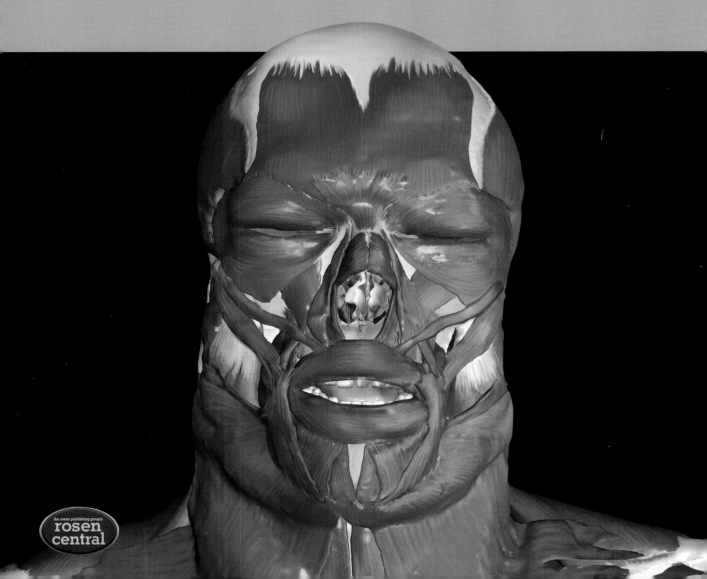

the rosen publishing group's
rosen central

Editor's Note

The idea for the illustrations in this book originated in 1986 with the Vesalius Project at Colorado State University's Department of Anatomy and Neurobiology. There, a team of scientists and illustrators dreamed of turning conventional two-dimensional anatomical illustrations into three-dimensional computer images that could be rotated and viewed from any angle, for the benefit of students of medicine and biology. In 1988 this dream became the Visible Human Project™, under the sponsorship of the National Library of Medicine in Bethesda, Maryland. A grant was awarded to the University of Colorado School of Medicine, and in 1993 the first work of dissection and scanning began on the body of a Texas convict who had been executed by lethal injection. The process was repeated on the body of a Maryland woman who had died of a heart attack. Applying the latest techniques of computer graphics, the scientific team was able to create a series of three-dimensional digital images of the human body so beautiful and startlingly accurate that they seem more in the realm of art than science. On the computer screen, muscles, bones, and organs of the body can be turned and viewed from any angle, and layers of tissue can be electronically peeled away to reveal what lies underneath. In reproducing these digital images in two-dimensional print form, the editors at Rosen have tried to preserve the three-dimensional character of the work by showing organs of the body from different perspectives and using illustrations that progressively reveal deeper layers of anatomical structure.

Published in 2002 by The Rosen Publishing Group, Inc.
29 East 21st Street, New York, NY 10010

Digital anatomy images published by arrangement with Anatographica, LLC.
216 East 49th Street, New York, NY 10017

First Edition

Library of Congress Cataloging-in-Publication Data

Oleksy, Walter G., 1930–
The head and neck: learning how we use our muscles / Walter Oleksy. — 1st ed.
p. cm. — (The 3-D library of the human body)
Includes bibliographical references and index.
Summary: A discussion of the anatomy of the head and neck, the muscles and skeletal structure that allow movement, and the vitally important sense organs.
ISBN 0-8239-3531-0 (lib. bdg.)
1. Head—Anatomy—Juvenile literature. 2. Neck—Anatomy—Juvenile literature. [1. Head. 2. Neck. 3. Senses and sensation.]
I. Title. II. Series.
QM535 .O43 2001
611'.91—dc21
                                                                    2001002821

Manufactured in the United States of America

CONTENTS

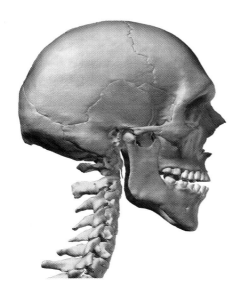

PREFACE
ANDREAS VESALIUS

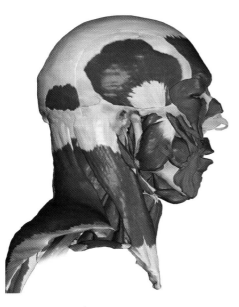

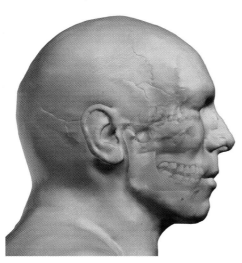

The Flemish physician Andreas Vesalius (1514–1564) was the founder of the modern science of anatomy and was as much a part of the Scientific Revolution as Nicolas Copernicus was. Vesalius was born in Brussels, Belgium, and he came from a long line of physicians and pharmacists. His father was court apothecary to Charles V of Spain, the Holy Roman Emperor. Vesalius studied medicine at the University of Louvain and the University of Paris and obtained his medical degree from the University of Padua in 1537. He became very interested in anatomy.

At the time, most doctors and scholars accepted the work of the ancient Greek physician Galen (AD 130–200) as the final authority on human anatomy. But Greek and Roman law had prohibited the dissection of human beings. Galen had really drawn analogies about human anatomy from his dissection of pigs and apes. Vesalius believed that it was necessary to examine real cadavers to learn about the human body. He revived the practice of human dissection, in spite of the continuing prohibition of it by the Catholic Church. As he progressed, Vesalius began to find more and more errors in the work of Galen and came to realize that the ancient physician's work was based on the dissection of animals, not humans. In one famous demonstration at the dissecting table, Vesalius proved that men and women have the same number of ribs. Because in the biblical story of Adam and Eve, Eve was created from one of Adam's ribs, it had been widely believed that men had one less rib than women. Vesalius destroyed that misconception.

In 1543, at the age of twenty-nine, Vesalius published his major work on human anatomy, *De Humani Corporis Fabrica* (*The Structure of the Human Body*). The book included more than 200 anatomical illustrations, many of them prepared by Jan Stephan van Calcar, a student of the great artist Titian. This was the first truly accurate presentation of human anatomy. It corrected many of Galen's errors, such as the Greeks' belief that blood could flow between the ventricles of the heart, and that the mandible, or jaw bone, was composed of more than one bone. The illustrations of the muscles in particular were extremely precise. The seven volumes of *De Humani Corporis Fabrica* established an accurate understanding of human anatomy as the basis for all medical practice and healing. Vesalius became court physician to Charles V of Spain and later served as physician to his son, Philip II.

Vesalius's attack on Galen, however, as well as his advocacy of human dissection, earned him many enemies among conservative physicians and Catholic clergy. He was continually accused of body snatching, dissection, and heresy. In 1564 he was accused of murder for dissecting a Spanish nobleman who, his accusers claimed, was still alive. The relatives of the nobleman also accused Vesalius of atheism. He might have been executed had he not enjoyed the protection of the Spanish king Philip II, who reduced his sentence to a pilgrimage of penitence to the Holy Land. Unfortunately, on the return voyage his vessel was severely damaged by a storm, and though he was rescued from the sea, Vesalius died shortly thereafter.

1
THE MUSCLES

There are about 650 skeletal muscles in the human body, making up nearly half of the body weight of an adult. Muscles are fleshy tissues that contract (shorten) or relax (lengthen) in response to nerve impulses. Skeletal muscles are those that are connected to bones and therefore control the basic motions of the body. They allow the body to move in complicated ways, such as leaping up to slam-dunk a basketball, or performing a ballerina's pirouette, or just chewing, swallowing, and talking.

Muscles are not able to stretch, but they contract and relax under stimulus from nerve cells attached to them. Each muscle is made of hundreds to thousands of individual muscle cells. In order to contract, muscle fibers must be stimulated by nerve impulses sent through motor neurons, which are nerve cells designed specifically to control muscular movement. A single motor neuron may stimulate either a few muscle fibers or hundreds of them. A motor neuron along with all the fibers it stimulates is called a motor unit.

Nerve impulses originate in the brain and then run down the spine. From the spinal cord, they branch out to all parts of the body. When a muscle contracts, it pulls on one of the bones to which it is attached. Bone is a type of connective tissue that has evolved to be very hard and strong but lightweight. It is made up of cells and protein fibers

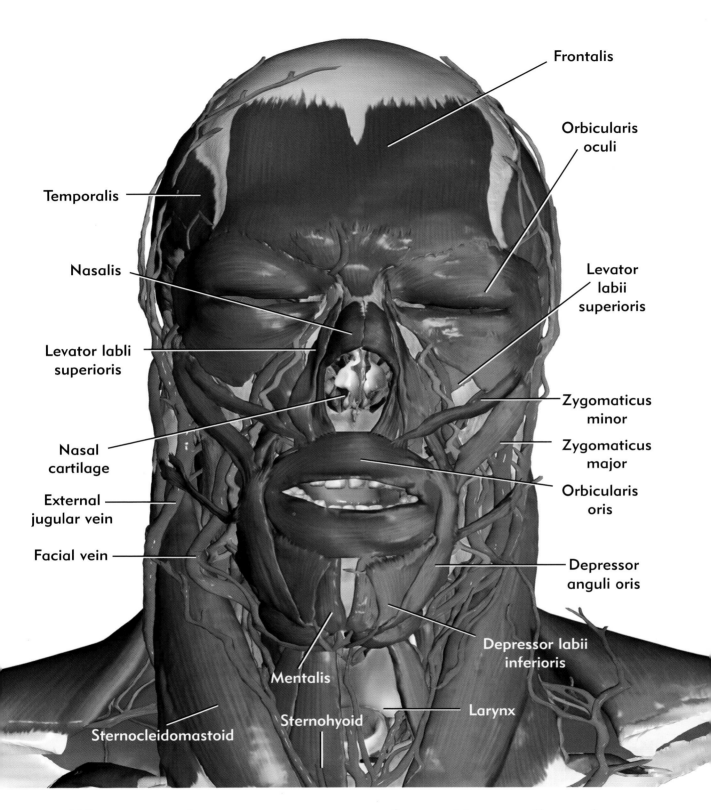

Frontalis

Orbicularis oculi

Temporalis

Nasalis

Levator labii superioris

Levator labli superioris

Zygomaticus minor

Nasal cartilage

Zygomaticus major

External jugular vein

Orbicularis oris

Facial vein

Depressor anguli oris

Depressor labii inferioris

Mentalis

Larynx

Sternocleidomastoid

Sternohyoid

When we speak, we use one or more of over thirty small muscles.
Other muscles control the movement of our eyes and our neck, and
our facial expressions.

interwoven into a hard, calcified matrix that is porous, that is, full of small cavities—empty spaces that reduce its weight. Many facial muscles are not attached to bones but to each other, or to the skin. Which muscle contracts when, and with what force, is controlled and coordinated by the brain in the case of voluntary movements.

When we smile, frown, or open our mouths to speak or shout, we use one or more of over thirty small facial muscles. Most facial muscles are in pairs, one on each side of the face. The muscles pull on the skin of the face, changing its shape. Larger muscles move the head and keep it upright. They also close the lower jaw when we eat or speak.

The Face

Seven muscles in the front of the face do different things. The frontalis muscle pulls the scalp forward to wrinkle the forehead and raise the eyebrows. The orbicularis oculi muscle surrounds the eye sockets and closes the eyes. The levator labii superioris muscle raises the upper lip and flares the nostrils when we demonstrate disgust for something.

The orbicularis oris muscle surrounds the mouth and closes the lips. The depressor anguli oris muscle draws the corners of the mouth downward in an expression of a grimace. The depressor labii inferioris muscle pulls the lower lip downward in a pout. The semispinalis capitis muscle is a broad, sheetlike muscle that extends up from the vertebrae in the neck and thorax to the occipital bone. It extends the head, bends it to one side, and rotates it.

The platysma muscle in the side of the chin and neck draws the lower lip and corner of the mouth sideways and down, partially opening the mouth, as in an expression of doubt, rejection, surprise, or fright. It is a broad sheet of muscle arising from the pectoral (chest) and deltoid (shoulder) muscles and rises over the clavicle (collarbone), proceeding upward in a slanting manner along the sides of the neck.

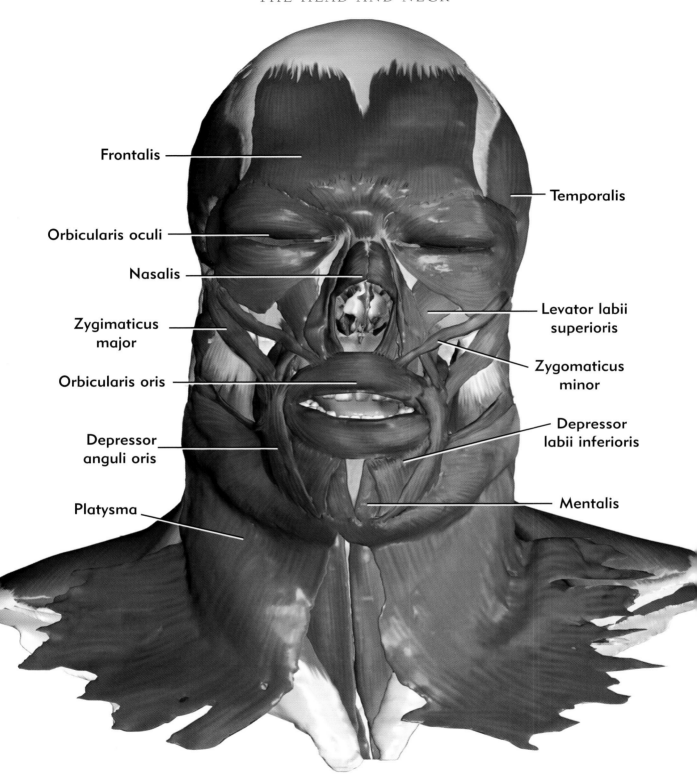

Frontalis

Temporalis

Orbicularis oculi

Nasalis

Levator labii superioris

Zygimaticus major

Zygomaticus minor

Orbicularis oris

Depressor labii inferioris

Depressor anguli oris

Mentalis

Platysma

The muscles in the face each have different functions. For example, the orbicularis oculi muscle surrounds the eye sockets and closes the eyes.

All skeletal muscles have the same basic features. The center of the muscle, called the belly, is attached to bones or other structures at each end. But the shape, power, and mobility of individual muscles depend on how their fascicles are arranged. Fascicles are bundles of muscle fibers. Their number and orientation determine how powerful muscles are and in what direction they will contract or relax.

There are three types of muscles in the head and neck: parallel muscles, pennate muscles, and circular muscles. Parallel muscles have fascicles arranged parallel to the long axis of the muscle. They can be fusiform, with a fleshy belly, such as the biceps femoris in the upper arm. Or they can be straplike, such as the sartorius in the thigh.

Pennate muscles have fascicles arranged obliquely (at an angle, neither parallel nor perpendicular) to a tendon running along the center of the muscle. These muscles can be unipennate, with fascicles attached to one side of the tendon, such as the extensor digitorum longus in the lower leg. Bipennate muscles have fascicles attached like feathers to both sides of the central tendon, such as the rectus femoris in the thigh. Multipennate muscles are those with many bipennate units, such as the deltoid muscle in the shoulder.

Circular muscles are those with concentric (circular or spherical) rows of fascicles. They form a sphincter muscle that controls the closing of external body openings, such as the orbicularis oculi muscle around the eyes. The sphincter muscle contracts when the eyelids close. Six pairs of muscles control the almost constant movements of the eyeballs.

A sphincter muscle also forms a large part of the lips. Seven pairs of muscles control movements of the mouth that turn the corners of the mouth up or down, or in and out. Movements of the jaw are controlled by four different pairs of muscles. Of these, the temporalis and masseter muscles are very powerful sets of muscles that raise the lower jaw and close the mouth during eating and chewing.

Muscle Talk

It takes seventeen muscles to make a smile, but forty-three muscles to make a frown. The smallest muscle in the human body is the stapedius muscle in the ear, just 0.05 inch (0.13 centimeter) long. It activates the stirrup, the small bone that sends vibrations from the eardrum to the inner ear. The fastest-reacting muscle in the human body is the orbicularis oculi, which encircles the eye and closes the eyelid. It contracts in less than 0.01 second.

The Side and the Back of the Head

Other muscles at the side and back of the head and neck control additional facial expressions and support and move the head and neck.

The risorius muscle pulls the corners of the lips laterally (sideways) when we smile. The zygomaticus muscle pulls the corners of the mouth up and out when we smile or laugh. The corrugator supercilii muscle wrinkles the brow when we frown. The buccinator (cheek muscle) pushes the cheeks inward when we suck on something, and also forces food inward between the teeth during chewing.

As mentioned, two powerful muscles, the temporalis and masseter, raise the lower jaw to close the mouth. The occipitalis muscle, at the back of the skull, is linked to the frontalis by a flat tendon, the galea aponeurotica, the muscle that covers the upper part of the skull. Attached to the frontal and occipital bellies (muscles on the brow at the front and on the upper back of the head), it moves the scalp freely

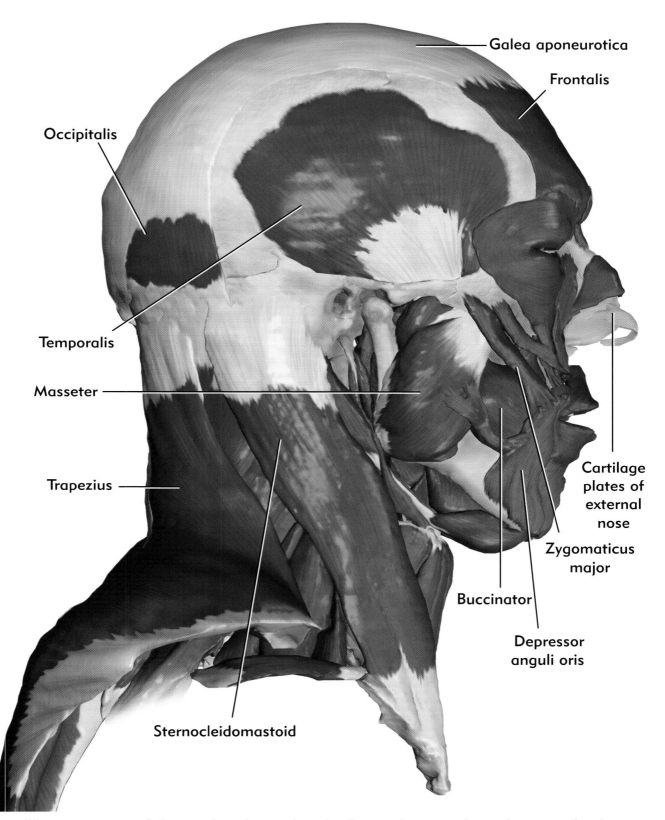

Galea aponeurotica

Frontalis

Occipitalis

Temporalis

Masseter

Trapezius

Sternocleidomastoid

Cartilage plates of external nose

Zygomaticus major

Buccinator

Depressor anguli oris

The two powerful muscles that raise the lower jaw to close the mouth, the temporalis and the masseter, are clearly visible in this image.

over the underlying skull bone. The occipital and frontal bellies work together with this muscle to draw back the scalp, raise the eyebrows, and wrinkle the forehead in an expression of surprise.

The sternocleidomastoid muscles flex the head, pulling it toward the chest. These are the long muscles in the side of the neck that extend up from the thorax to the base of the skull behind the ears. When this muscle on one side of the head contracts, the face turns to the opposite side. When both muscles contract, the head bends toward the chest.

While a sternocleidomastoid muscle acting individually rotates the head to one side, the trapezius muscle has an opposing action, pulling the head and shoulders backward. It is a flat, triangular muscle that covers the back of the neck, shoulders, and thorax.

Lying deep in the neck on either side are the cervical plexus muscles. They are connected to the front branches of the first four cervical nerves. In the back of the neck is the splenius capitis muscle. It is a broad, straplike muscle that connects the base of the skull to the vertebrae and the upper thorax. Acting singly, a splenius capitis muscle causes the head to rotate and bend toward one side. Together, these muscles bring the head into an upright position.

How Muscle Fibers Contract

Almost all movements of the body result from muscle contraction. Even when a person is at rest or asleep, muscle fibers contract to maintain muscle tone and good health. Muscle activity generates heat, which is vital in maintaining normal body temperature.

An individual skeletal muscle fiber is from one-sixteenth of an inch to twelve inches (one millimeter to thirty centimeters) long. As we have said, in order to contract or shorten, muscle fibers have to be stimulated by nerve impulses sent through motor neurons or

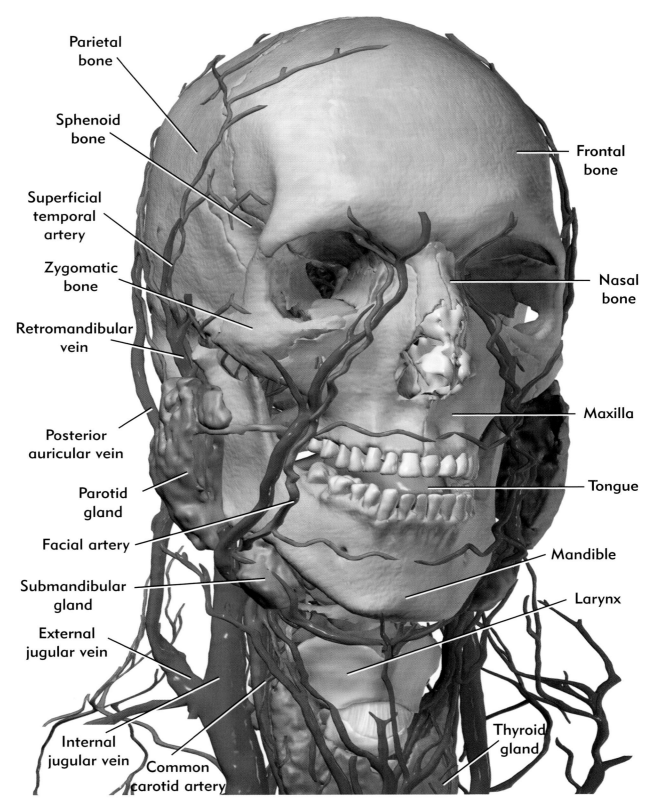

Parietal bone

Sphenoid bone

Superficial temporal artery

Zygomatic bone

Retromandibular vein

Posterior auricular vein

Parotid gland

Facial artery

Submandibular gland

External jugular vein

Internal jugular vein

Common carotid artery

Frontal bone

Nasal bone

Maxilla

Tongue

Mandible

Larynx

Thyroid gland

Major arteries and vessels carry blood through the neck and head and into the brain.

nerves. When a motor neuron reaches a muscle fiber, it fits into a hollow on the surface of the muscle fiber. When a nerve impulse reaches the end of the motor neuron, a neurotransmitter, a chemical called acetylcholine, is released. This chemical crosses the small gap between the motor neuron and the muscle fiber and attaches to receptors on the membrane of the muscle fiber. This sets off an electrical charge that travels rapidly from one end of the muscle fiber to the other, causing it to contract.

2

THE SKELETAL STRUCTURE

The skeleton is the bony framework that supports the body and gives it shape. The human adult skeleton has 206 bones joined by ligaments and tendons, tough bands of flexible tissue that hold the bones together and help support the organs of the body. The attached muscles exert force on these bones as if they were levers, enabling us to walk, raise our arms, and bend over.

The skeleton has two main parts: the axial skeleton and the appendicular skeleton. The axial skeleton consists of the skull, spine, ribs, and sternum (breastbone), and includes 80 bones. The appendicular skeleton includes two limb girdles (the shoulders and pelvis) and their attached limb bones. This part of the skeletal system contains 126 bones.

The head houses the brain, an organ that is the body's control system. The brain, a jelly-like substance that weighs about three pounds in an adult, is protected by the skull and its cranial bones. The head also houses the sensory organs for seeing, hearing, smelling, and tasting. These organs are the eyes, the ears, the nose, and the tongue. Their proximity to the brain ensures rapid processing of the complex information they gather from the environment.

The brain itself is divided into three parts: the brain stem, which is an extension of the spinal cord; the forebrain, which consists mainly of the

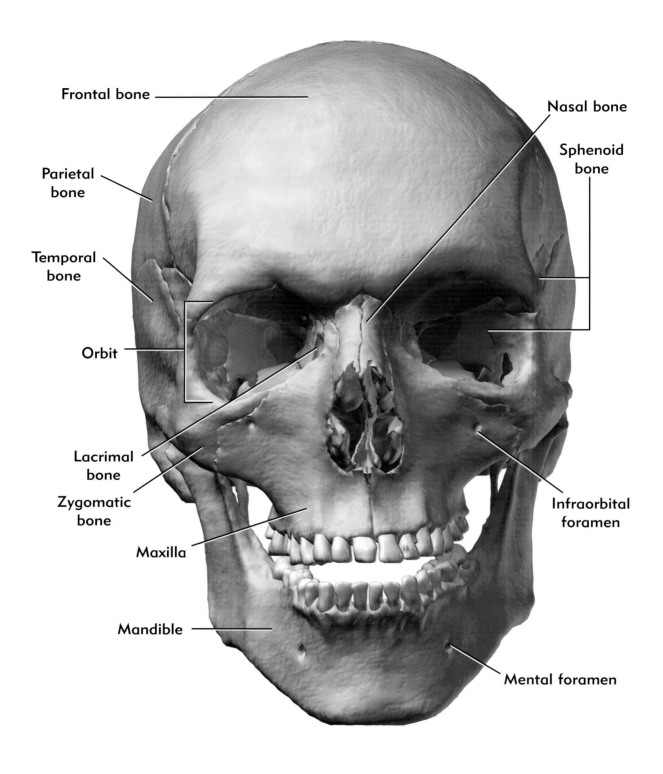

Frontal bone

Nasal bone

Sphenoid bone

Parietal bone

Temporal bone

Orbit

Lacrimal bone

Zygomatic bone

Maxilla

Infraorbital foramen

Mandible

Mental foramen

The skull encases and protects the brain and provides a surface to which the muscles of the head and neck are attached.

cerebrum; and the cerebellum. The forebrain and the cerebrum are divided into two hemispheres, which are linked by a thick band of nerve fibers known as the corpus callosum. The wiring system of the brain is "crossed," that is, the right cerebral hemisphere controls the left side of the body, and vice versa. Three layers of connective tissue membranes, known as meninges, along with spaces filled with cerebrospinal fluid, surround and cushion the brain from shocks or injury when the head hits something.

The Skull

The human skull is the bony section of the head. It encases and protects the brain and provides attachments for the muscles of the head and neck. The skull consists of two sets of bones: cranial bones and facial bones. They protect and support the organs that are responsible for the five basic senses: sight, hearing, smell, taste, and touch. The front of the skull also features two orbits, which are cuplike sockets or hollow places that hold the eyes.

In the bones of the forehead and the cheeks are air-filled spaces called sinuses. The sinuses in the bones that surround the nasal cavity, the hole in the middle of the face, are called the paranasal sinuses. They are cavities in the bones of the face that are lined with mucous membranes. The mucus produced in the sinuses drains into the nasal cavity to moisturize and warm the air as it flows into the respiratory tract. When drainage from the paranasal sinuses is blocked, such as during a cold, the sinuses often become affected and cause headaches or other discomforts.

Most of the nose is composed of soft, springy cartilage, but the base of the nose is bone. The maxilla is the bone of the upper jaw. The mandible is the bone of the lower jaw. The mandible is one of the few bones in the head that can move. The muscles that move it are anchored to the cheekbones and the sides of the skull.

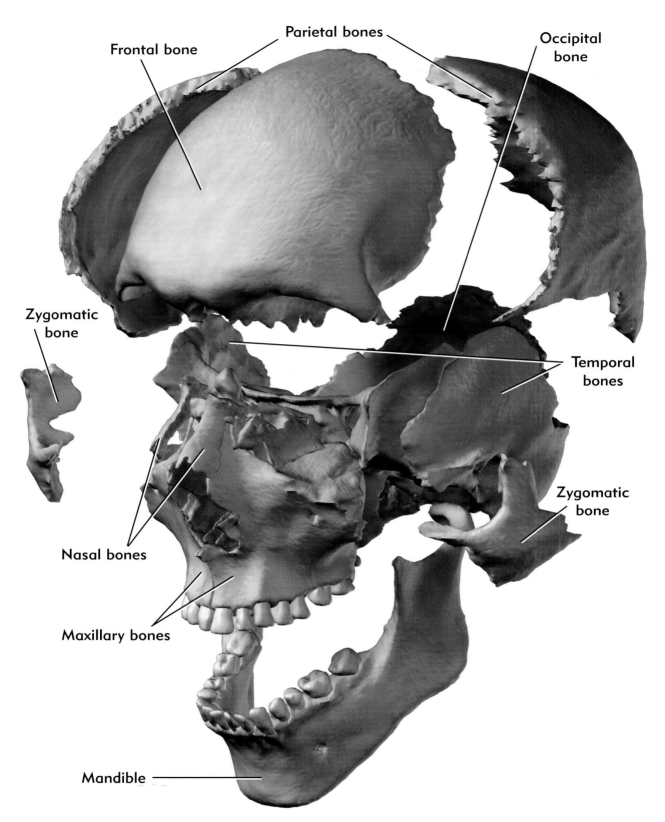

Frontal bone

Parietal bones

Occipital bone

Zygomatic bone

Temporal bones

Zygomatic bone

Nasal bones

Maxillary bones

Mandible

The skull houses the cranial and facial bones, which protect and support the brain and the organs that enable us to see, hear, smell, and taste.

The part of the skull that encloses the brain is the cranium, or "brain-box." Its eight bones are thin and flat. Interlocking at their joints, they cannot move. The frontal bone forms the forehead and the upper part of the eye sockets. Two parietal bones form the sides and upper portion of the cranium.

Under the parietal bones are two temporal bones, one on each side of the skull. They join the parietal bone along the squamosal suture. Temporal bones form parts of the sides and the base of the cranium. The occipital bone forms the back of the cranium. The temporal bones house the internal structures of the ear. They have depressions, called the mandibular fossae, where the mandible, the bone of the lower jaw, attaches to the temporal bones.

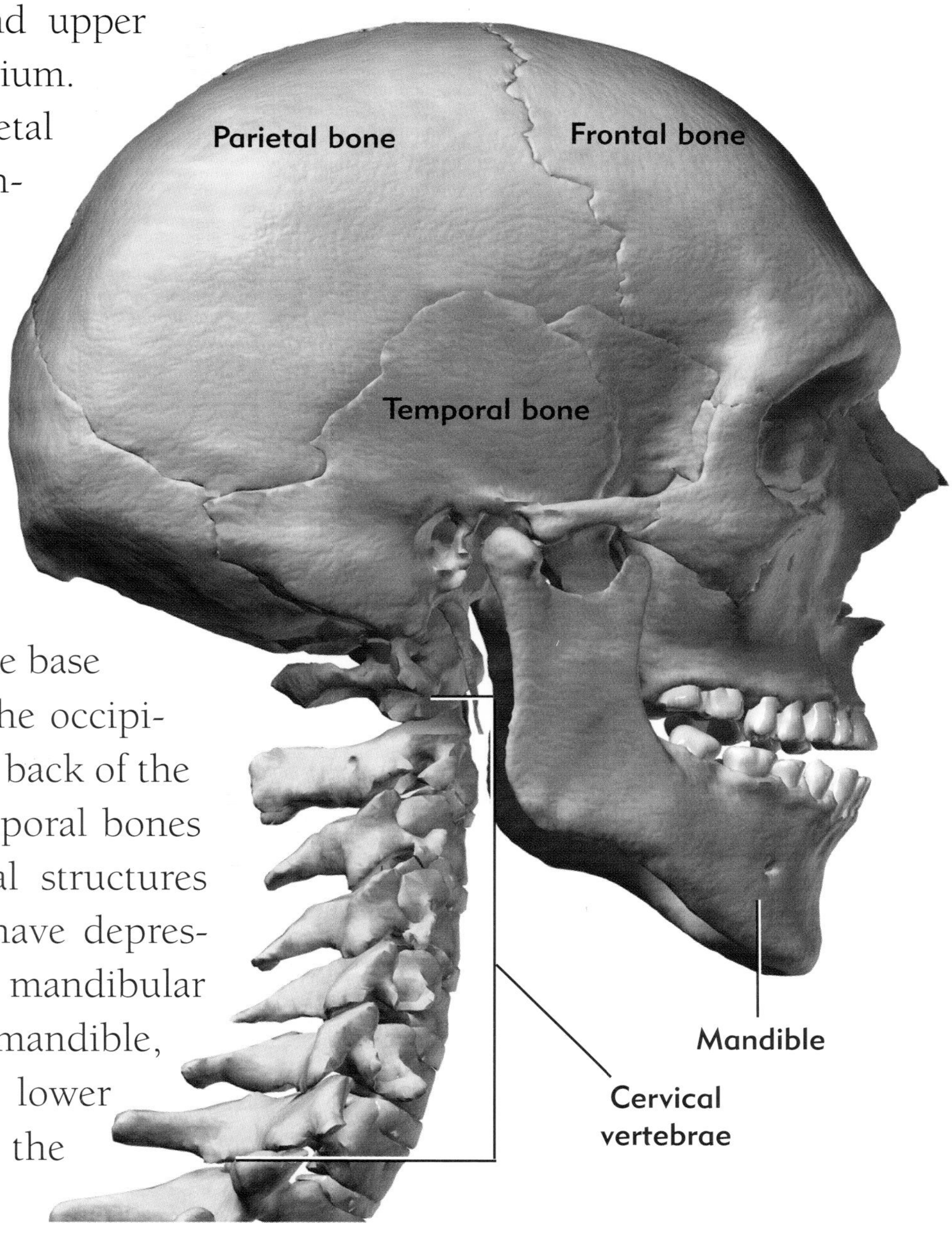

Parietal bone

Frontal bone

Temporal bone

Mandible

Cervical vertebrae

The cervical vertebrae of the neck support the head and enable it to turn from side to side and up and down.

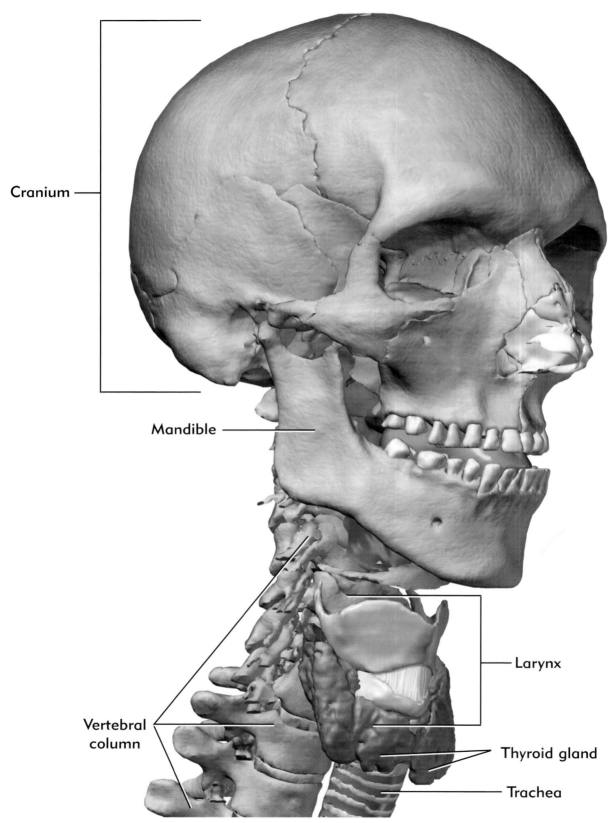

Cranium

Mandible

Larynx

Vertebral
column

Thyroid gland

Trachea

The larynx and trachea are clearly visible in this view of the head
and neck.

Teeth are hard structures in the upper and lower jaws that aid in chewing food and in the process of speaking clearly. They also give shape to the face. The hardest substance in the human body, even harder than bone, is enamel, one of the four kinds of tissue that make up a tooth. Enamel covers the crown of the tooth, the area above the gum line. A bony material, the cementum, covers the root, which fits into the jaw socket and is joined to it with membranes. At the heart of

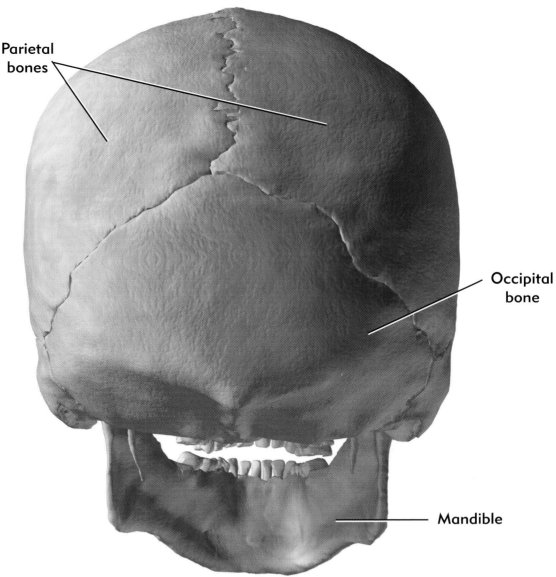

The occipital bone forms the rear and floor of the cranium and is only visible in a posterior view of the skull.

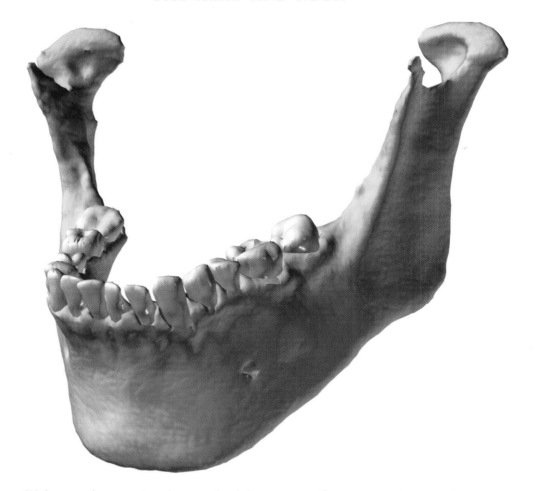

The mandible, or lower jawbone, holds some of our teeth and is controlled by some of the most powerful muscles of the head.

each tooth is living pulp, which contains nerves, connective tissues, blood vessels, and lymphatic tissue. When we get a toothache, it is the nerve inside the pulp that hurts.

There are fourteen bones in the face. As mentioned, some facial bones contain hollow, air-filled spaces known as sinuses. The main function of the sinuses is to reduce the weight of the skull and to provide sound quality for the voice.

Bones that are not considered part of the skull but that are associated with it include the bones of the middle ear and the hyoid bone. Three auditory bones inside each middle ear cavity transmit vibrations from the ear drum to receptors in the inner ear. Those bones are the incus, the stapes, and the malleus. The horseshoe-shaped hyoid bone is suspended by ligaments from the lower portions of the temporal bones. It lies in the neck just above the larynx (voice box). It plays an important part in swallowing, supporting the tongue and larynx.

A skull fracture is a break in one or more of the skull bones, caused by a blow to the head. Because the skull is very strong, most fractures close by themselves and cause no complications. Young people at play without helmets may suffer skull fractures by falling from bicycles or skateboards, or from being hit by bats or balls. Anyone suffering a violent blow to the head, especially if it causes unconsciousness, should see a doctor because skull fractures can result in brain injury.

The Neck

The neck supports the head, enables it to move, and provides a link between the head and the trunk of the body. Supporting the neck are seven cervical vertebrae; the top two allow the head to turn from side to side and up and down.

No Brainers

The brain requires large amounts of stored energy for thinking. This is why a person may feel as tired after studying hard as he or she would after a strenuous sport activity or a physical workout. One of the hardest-working parts of the body, the brain doesn't even stop working immediately after a person dies. It continues to send out electrical signals for about thirty-seven hours after death.

Cervical vertebrae

Thoracic vertebrae

Lumbar vertebrae

Sacrum

Coccyx

The neck contains the larynx, or voice box, composed mostly of muscles and cartilage that are bound together by elastic tissues. The thyroid cartilage was named for the thyroid gland that covers its lower part. This cartilage is the shieldlike structure that protrudes in the front of the neck and is called the Adam's apple. It is usually more prominent in males than in females because of the effect of male sex hormones on the development of the larynx.

The trachea, or windpipe, begins immediately below the larynx and runs down the center of the front part of the neck, ending behind the upper part of the sternum. It then divides to form two branches that enter the lung cavities. The trachea is made up of fibrous and elastic tissues and smooth muscle with about twenty rings of cartilage that help keep the trachea open during extreme neck movements.

The spine is the body's backbone, a strong, curved, rodlike series of thirty-three bones called vertebrae that support the main parts of the body in an upright position. Supporting the skull on the spine is the first vertebrae, or atlas, at a joint that allows for nodding and other head and neck movements. It is called the atlas because in Greek mythology, after leading the Titans in an unsuccessful war against the Olympians,

The spinal column, or backbone, is a strong but flexible chain of bones.

the god Atlas was condemned to hold the sky on his shoulders for all eternity. This was the mythological explanation for what holds up the sky.

The first vertebrae has a ringlike socket into which fits a peg from the second vertebrae, called the axis. Two rounded bumps under the skull fit into the hollows on the atlas and allow nodding movements. The muscles of the posterior of the neck, such as the splenius capitis and semispinalis capitis, assisted by the trapezius, support the head by pulling it back to keep it from falling forward.

The spinal cord is the brain's main link with the rest of the body. It is a cable about seventeen inches (forty-three centimeters) long that descends from the brain stem to the lumbar part of the back. Through thirty-one pairs of spinal nerves, the spinal cord is connected to the rest of the body and relays information from the sensory nerves to the brain, and from the brain to the motor nerves. The brain and nerves make up the body's nervous system.

Injuries to the head and neck can cause paralysis. In 1995, Christopher Reeve, the athletic actor who played Superman in the movies, fell from his horse and landed on his head. The first and second cervical vertebrae, those closest to the skull, had been shattered. Severe damage to his spinal cord left Reeve a quadriplegic, unable to move his arms and legs. Scientists and doctors are experimenting to repair damaged or severed spinal cords and restore two-way communication up and down the spine.

Intervertebral disks

The intervertebral disks are pads of cartilage with a jelly-like filling that cushions the spinal column during movement.

27

3
THE SENSORY ORGANS

The sensory organs of the head and neck enable us to taste, hear, smell, see, and feel general sensations such as heat, cold, pain, and pressure.

The Organ of Taste

Both taste and smell are chemical senses stimulated by chemical molecules. Tastes are detected by special structures called gustatory cayculi, or taste buds. Humans have about 10,000 taste buds, mainly on the tongue, but a few are at the back of the throat and on the palate, on the top of the mouth.

There are four types of taste buds, each sensitive to a different taste: sweet, salty, sour, and bitter. Each taste receptor is most highly concentrated in certain regions of the tongue's surface. Sweet receptors are mostly on the tip of the tongue, sour receptors are mainly along the sides of the tongue, salt receptors are most common in the tip (apex) and upper front portion of the tongue, and bitter receptors are located toward the back of the tongue.

The tongue's many muscles allow for sucking, swallowing, and making sounds to produce speech and song. Most of the tongue consists of closely interlaced muscles arranged in pairs so that the left and right sides of the tongue have independent sets of muscles.

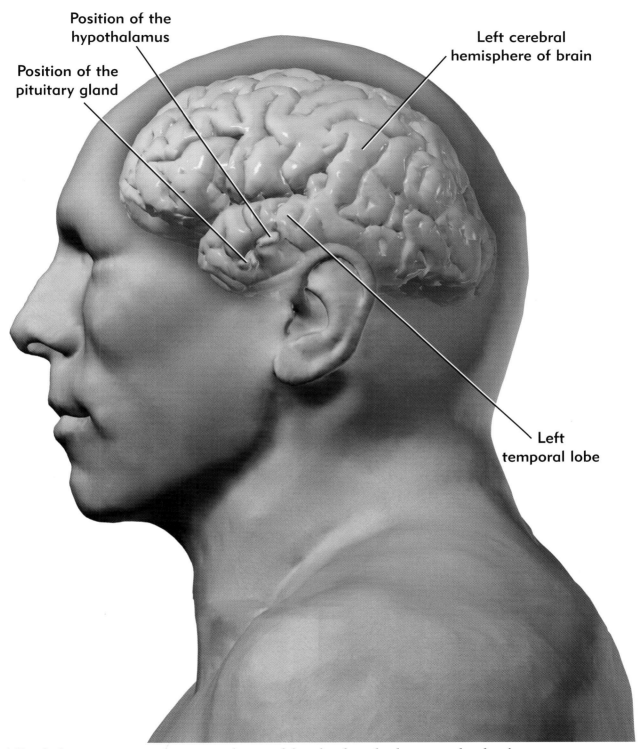

Position of the
hypothalamus

Position of the
pituitary gland

Left cerebral
hemisphere of brain

Left
temporal lobe

All of the sensory organs are located in the head, close to the brain.
This permits us to analyze sensory data rapidly.

It Makes Sense

The human nose can distinguish between 50,000 different smells. Every three to four hours, our nostrils switch duty; one keeps smelling and breathing while the other rests. Ear wax comes from a combination of body oil and sweat. If you stand on your head while swallowing, your food would not go down but up, because muscles in the esophagus would still pull the food into your stomach.

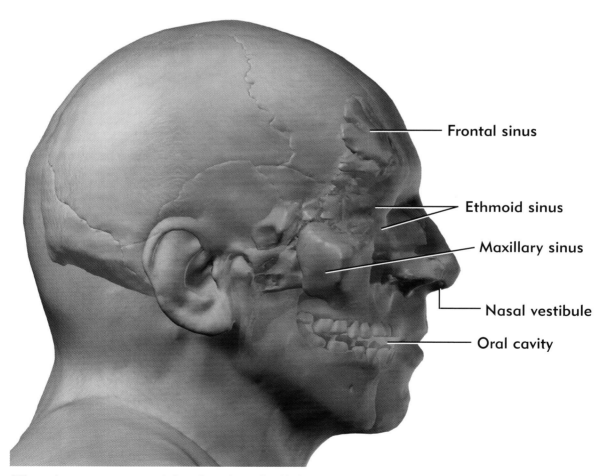

- Frontal sinus
- Ethmoid sinus
- Maxillary sinus
- Nasal vestibule
- Oral cavity

The sinuses are cavities in the skull bone surrounding the nasal passages. They warm and moisten the air before it is drawn into the lungs.

The tongue is anchored to the floor of the mouth and at the rear of the mouth by muscles attached to a spiky outgrowth at the base of the skull. The tongue's muscles are attached to the lower jaw and to the hyoid bone deep in the muscles at the back of the tongue and above the larynx.

The Organ for Hearing

The ear, an organ for both hearing and balance, consists of three parts: the outer ear, the middle ear, and the inner ear. The outer and middle ear mainly collect and transmit sound. The inner ear analyzes sound waves and contains an apparatus that maintains the body's balance.

The outer ear is the part that is visible and is made of folds of skin and cartilage. It leads into the ear canal, which is closed at the inner end by the eardrum. Sound enters the ear through the ear canal and strikes the tympanic membrane. Resulting vibrations affect three bones in the middle ear—the malleus, incus, and staples—that in turn pass the vibrations into the cochlea to the organ of Corti. Impulses from this organ travel to the brain to be interpreted as sound.

The middle ear or tympanic cavity is a small, irregular, laterally compressed space within the temporal bone. It is filled with air sent from the nasal part of the pharynx through the auditory tube. It contains a chain of three tiny, movable bones called ossicles. They connect to the middle ear's medial wall and serve to convey the vibrations sent to the tympanic membrane across the cavity to the internal ear. Ossicles are the smallest bones in the human body.

The inner ear is a very delicate series of structures deep within the bones of the skull. It consists of a maze of winding passages called the labyrinth. The front is a tube that looks like a snail's shell and is concerned with hearing. The rear part is concerned with balance.

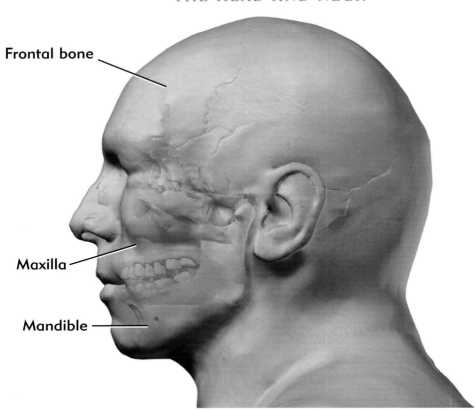

Frontal bone

Maxilla

Mandible

The structure of our facial bones determines what our faces look like, so much so that forensic (legal investigative) scientists can reconstruct faces from skulls.

Hearing is impaired and deafness may occur due to nerve deafness. Cilia on the sense receptors within the cochlea may have worn away, which may happen with age. Nerve deafness also may occur by listening frequently to loud sounds such as music amplified above 130 decibels.

The Organ of Smell

The nose is both the sensory organ that identifies smells and the main airway for the respiratory system. Inside the nose is the olfactory epithelium, a small patch of nerve cells with hairy projections. These are covered with receptors sensitive to the molecules of various substances in the air. There are about 10 million receptors in the nose, of at least twenty different types. When the receptors detect an odor, they send nerve signals along the olfactory nerve to the smell center in the brain. There the signal pattern is analyzed and the smell is identified.

The peripheral olfactory organ, or the organ of smell, consists of two parts: an outer part, the external nose that projects from the center of the face; and an inner part, the nasal cavity that is divided by a septum into right and left nasal chambers.

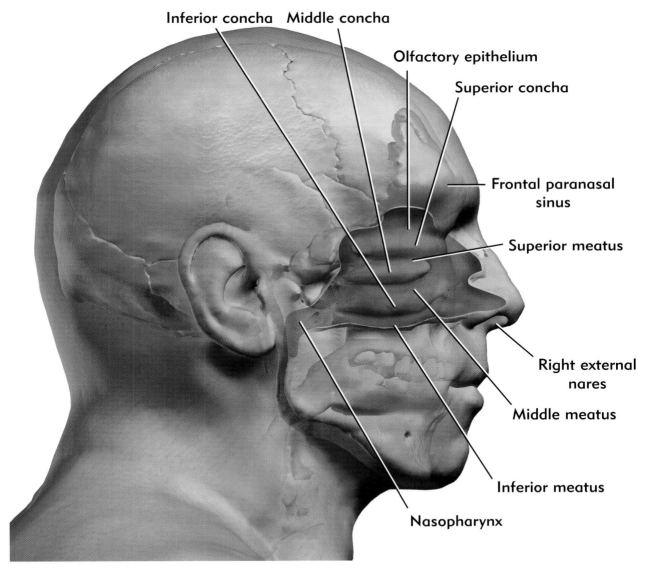

The nose not only enables us to smell, but it is also the main airway for the respiratory system.

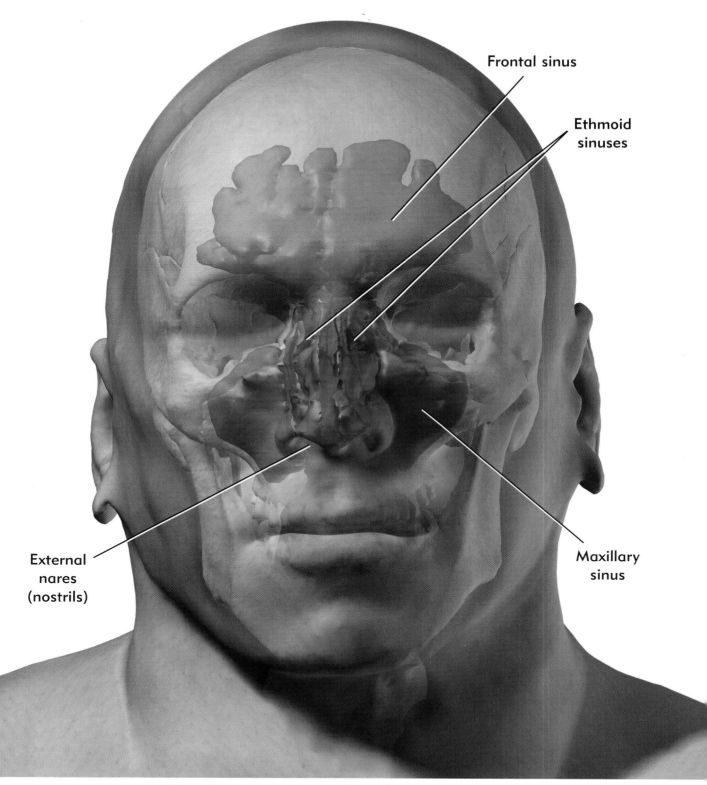

Frontal sinus

Ethmoid sinuses

Maxillary sinus

External nares (nostrils)

An anterior (front) view of the skull within the head showing the sinus cavities surrounding the nose.

The external nose is composed of bones and cartilage. Shaped like a pyramid, its upper angle, or root, connects directly with the forehead. Its free angle is termed the apex. Its base is perforated by two elliptical orifices, the nares, separated from each other by the columna.

The internal nose contains two nasal cavities, narrow canals with lateral walls separated from one another by a wall composed of bone and cartilage. Special cells in the narrow upper parts of the nasal cavities act as odor receptors. Nerves lead from these cells to the brain where impulses generated by the odor receptors are interpreted as smell.

As air passes through the nasal cavity with each inhalation, both gaseous and solid particles travel with it, causing stimulation of the olfactory bulbs. Impulses from these go to the brain where the sensation of smell occurs rapidly. During exhaling, the air passes below the olfactory bulbs.

The adenoids, two glands at the back of the nose above the tonsils, are made up of lymph node tissue that contains white cells to help the body fight infection. The adenoids tend to enlarge during early childhood, before the age of five or six, but usually disappear by puberty.

The Neck and Throat

Glossopharyngeal nerves, the ninth pair of cranial nerves, are associated with the tongue and pharynx. They are primarily sensory nerves. The fibers carry impulses to the brain from the lining of the pharynx, tonsils, and rear portion of the tongue. Fibers in the motor components aid in swallowing.

As food enters the back of the pharynx, a flap (the epiglottis) keeps it from entering the trachea and lungs. The food passes into the esophagus and down into the stomach. During swallowing, the soft palate and uvula are drawn upward, closing the portion of the pharynx opening to the nose, preventing food and fluid from entering the nasal cavity.

The esophagus is a muscular tube that carries food, as well as liquids, from the throat to the stomach for digestion after it has been chewed and chemically softened in the mouth. Food is forced downward to the stomach by powerful waves of muscle contractions passing through the walls of the esophagus. If the food tastes really awful or is poisonous, it may travel back by the action of the same muscles and be thrown out through the mouth, which is called vomiting.

The tonsils are a pair of oval-shaped organs in the back of the throat. They are part of the lymphatic system, which is important to the body's defense against infection. Like the adenoids at the base of the tongue, the tonsils protect against upper respiratory tract infections. They enlarge from birth to about seven years of age, then shrink.

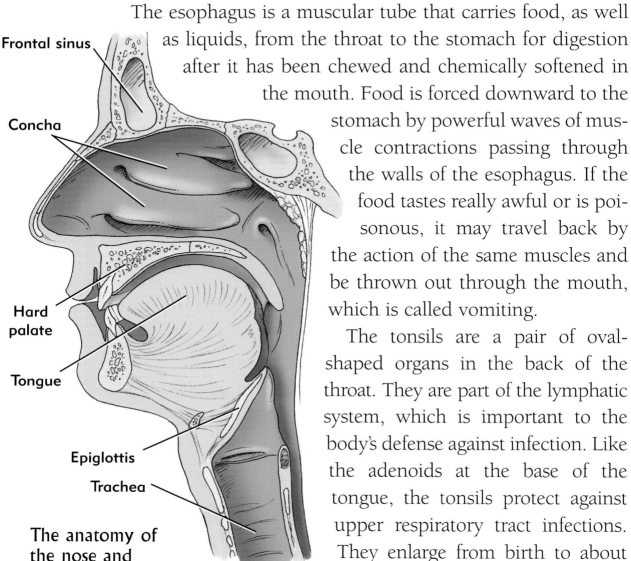

Frontal sinus

Concha

Hard palate

Tongue

Epiglottis

Trachea

The anatomy of the nose and throat

The Organs for Sight

The eyes, the sensory organs for vision, are at the front of the head, but the actual site where visual images are interpreted and created is at the back and sides of the brain. Light rays enter the eye through the cornea, an opening at the front of the eye. The light rays fall upon the retina, a layer of small, thin, light-sensitive cells at the back of the eyeball. The eye generates patterns of nerve signals and sends them to the brain.

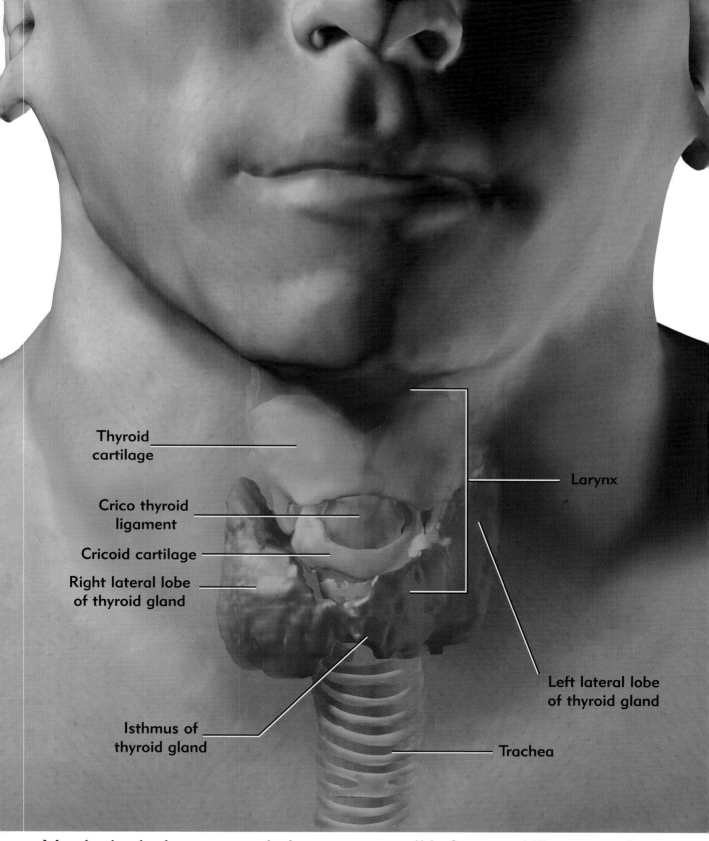

Thyroid cartilage

Crico thyroid ligament

Cricoid cartilage

Right lateral lobe of thyroid gland

Larynx

Left lateral lobe of thyroid gland

Isthmus of thyroid gland

Trachea

Muscles in the larynx, or voicebox, are responsible for our ability to speak.

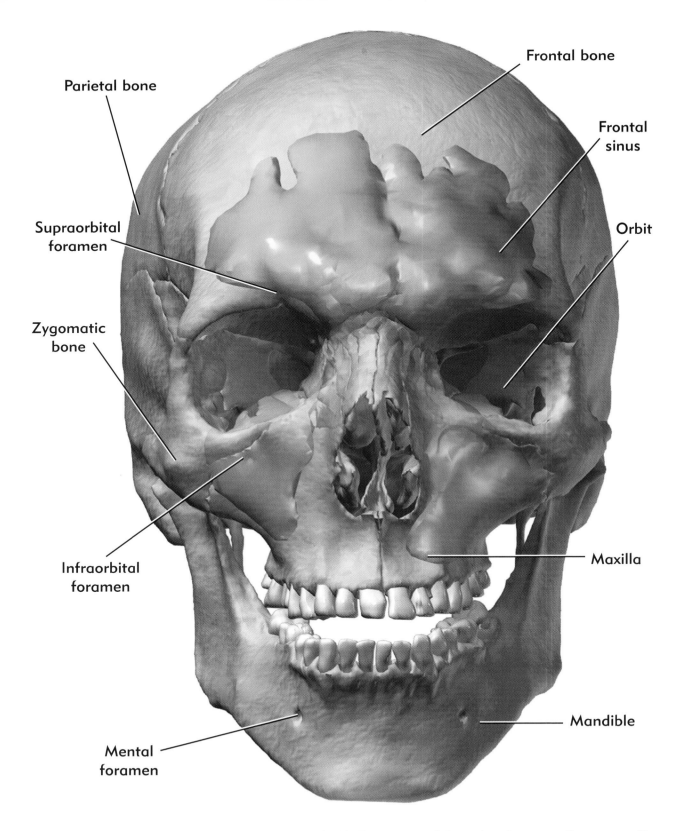

Parietal bone

Supraorbital
foramen

Zygomatic
bone

Infraorbital
foramen

Mental
foramen

Frontal bone

Frontal
sinus

Orbit

Maxilla

Mandible

An anterior (front) view of the skull. Foramina (singular foramen) are small
holes in the skull that provide passageways for blood vessels and nerves.

Nerve impulses from rods and cones, cells that respond to light and color, in the retinas of the eyes travel along the optic nerves, the second pair of the cranial nerves, to the optic chiasma, where they cross over each other. Rods are responsible for vision in dim light and create a black-and-white image. Cones create fine detail and are sensitive to color. Impulses from both eyes pass through the optic tracts to the striate cortex at the back of the brain. They end in the temporal lobe area, where right and left halves of the visual field merge.

Each eye sees objects from a slightly different angle. The fusion of the images from both eyes gives a three-dimensional effect called binocular or stereoscopic vision. Seeing an object and recognizing it involves image processing by cells in the retina and brain. The brain analyzes the optic signals and identifies information from them.

GLOSSARY

---

bone   Strong part of the body's skeletal structure composed mainly of calcium compounds.

brain   Organ in the skull that controls and coordinates the body's mental and physical actions.

cartilage   Tough, rubbery connective tissue that lines the ends of bones where they meet a joint.

cone   Receptor cell in the retina of the eye that detects color and provides visual sharpness.

fibers   Thin, threadlike structures in muscles that cause movement by shortening and lengthening.

inner ear   Part of the ear where balance is maintained and sound is transmitted.

joint   Connection between two or more bones.

larynx   Organ containing the vocal cords; also called the voice box.

ligaments   Fibrous tissues that hold bones together and connect joints.

mandible   Lower jaw.

middle ear   Air-filled cavity of the ear where sound is amplified.

organ   Major structural part of the body, usually a collection of tissues, that carries out a specific function.

ossicle   Small bone in the middle ear.

outer ear   Part of the ear containing the auditory canal.

pharynx   Passageway from the mouth to the throat for air movement and food intake.

retina   Light-sensitive layer that lines the inside of the rear of the eyeball, which contains the rods and the cones for sight.

rod   Receptor cell in the retina of the eye that detects motion but not color.

sinus   Cavity (hollow space) surrounding the nose, which warms inhaled air.

skeleton   Bony framework that supports the body and gives it shape.

vertebrae   Small, hollow bones making up the backbone that form a protective cover for the spinal cord.

FOR MORE INFORMATION

Organizations

National Health Information Center
P.O. Box 1133
Washington, DC 20013-1133
(800) 336-4797
e-mail: nhicinfo@health.org

Web Sites

Anatomy-Resources.Com
Web site: http://www.anatomy-resources.com
A Web site about the body that presents information with a sense
of humor.

BodyQuest
http://Library.thinkquest.org/10348/home.html
An illustrated Web site about human anatomy.

Gray's Anatomy of the Human Body
http://www.bartleby.com/107

A comprehensive Web site about the human body, with many illustrations. The site also has an online edition of *Anatomy of the Human Body*, published in 1918 by Henry Gray.

A Guided Tour of the Visible Human Project
http://www.madsci.org/~lynn/VH
An extensive Web site with more than 18,000 digitized sections of the body. It is the source of the digital images of the head and neck in this book.

HealthWeb
http://www.healthweb.org
An extensive Web site with links to many parts of anatomy.

Innerbody.com
http://www.innerbody.com/htm/body/html
Click on parts of the skeleton for illustrations and explanations of virtually every part of the human body.

Martindale's Health Science Guide: Anatomy & History Center
http://www-sci-lib.edu/HSG/MedicalAnatomy.html
A comprehensive Web site on every aspect of human anatomy.

Virtual Hospital: Atlas of Human Anatomy in Cross-Section
http://www.vh.org/Providers/Textbooks/HumanAnatomy/
    CrossSectionAtlas.html
Extensive Web site on human anatomy by doctor-instructors at the University of Iowa College of Medicine, in Iowa City, Iowa.

FOR FURTHER READING

Bender, Lionel. *The Human Body*. New York: Gloucester Press, 1989.

Biesty, Stephen, and Richard Platt. *Stephen Biesty's Incredible Body*. New York: Dorling Kindersley, 1998.

Burnie, David. *The Concise Encyclopedia of the Human Body*. New York: Dorling Kindersley, 1995.

Clayman, Charles, ed. *The Human Body: An Illustrated Guide to Its Structure, Function, and Disorders*. New York: Dorling Kindersley, 1995.

Guinness, Alma E., ed. *ABCs of the Human Body*. Pleasantville, NY: Reader's Digest, 1987.

Hewitt, Sally. *You and Your Body*. New York: Children's Press, 1999.

Parker, Steve. *How the Body Works*. Pleasantville, NY: Reader's Digest, 1994.

Perols, Sylvaine. *The Human Body*. New York: Scholastic, 1996.

Stonehouse, Bernard, ed. *The Way Your Body Works*. New York: Bonanza Books, 1985.

Whitfield, Philip. *The Human Body Explained*. New York: Henry Holt, 1995.

INDEX

About the Author

Walter Oleksy lives in Glenview, Illinois, with his adored dog Max, a black Labrador retriever–German shepherd mix. Oleksy is the author of more than fifty books for young readers and adults, including *The Nervous System* and *The Circulatory System* for the Rosen Publishing Group. He is a member of the Midwest Writers Association/American Society of Journalists and Authors, and the Association of Children's Book Writers and Illustrators. His Web site about his books is at http://home.earthlink.net/~waltmax/bio.html

Photo Credits

All digital images courtesy of Visible Productions by arrangement with Anatographica, LLC.

Series Design

Claudia Carlson

Layout

Tahara Hasan